THE CRAFT OF PAPER

Becca Heddle

Cover illustrated by **Julene Harrison**

Inside illustrations by **Venitia Dean**

OXFORD
UNIVERSITY PRESS

CONTENTS

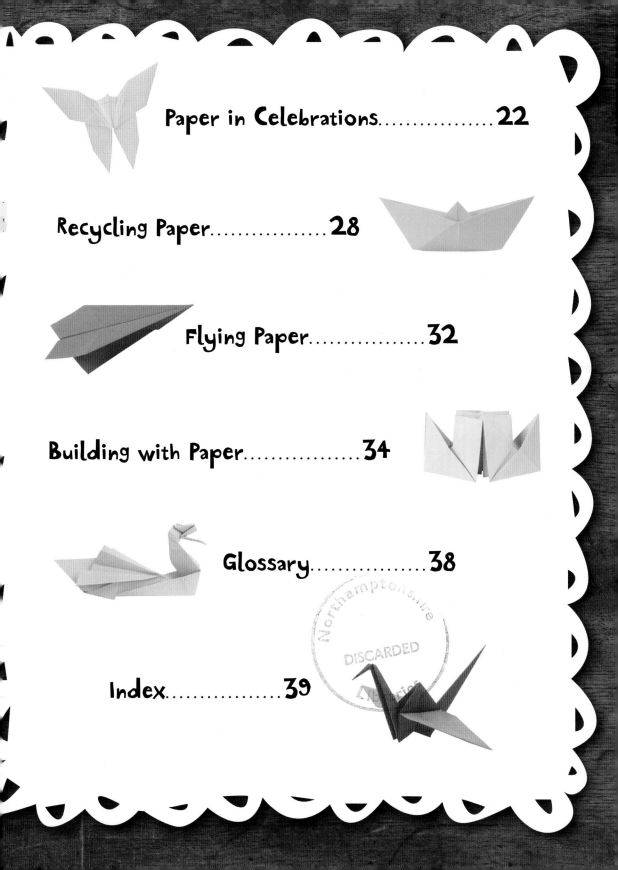

A BOOK ON PAPER

Hello. This book is on paper. Oh, sorry – I mean, of course it's printed on paper – most books are. But this book is also *about* paper. I bet you've never thought much about paper. You can find out more now – from how paper is made, to all the brilliant ways you can use it.

Here are just some of the different kinds of paper you might already know about.

The bobbly kind is used for painting.

You use this every day in school!

Cardboard is mainly used to make packaging, such as boxes or tubes.

Wallpaper is for covering walls – it can be printed or textured.

Wrapping paper can be plain, shiny or have patterns printed on it.

This paper is extra smooth. It's good for wrapping food.

Tissues are used for mopping things up.

The picture on this cake is printed on edible paper.

Magazines and leaflets are often made out of shiny paper.

Now let's have a look at paper in more detail ...

MAKING PAPER – BY HAND

Did you know that paper has been around for two thousand years? Until the 1800s, all paper was made by hand.

Imagine you work in a paper mill in the 1700s. These are your instructions for making paper by hand. It will take about 4–5 days from start to finish, and each step will be done by a different person.

1 First you need a lot of cotton rags. Beat them up with water until you have a mushy **pulp** that looks a bit like porridge. Mix this with more clean water and **starch** to make **stuff**.

2 Scoop up a layer of stuff using a wire **mesh** and shake it to even it out. Use a wooden frame called a deckle to give it a rectangular shape.

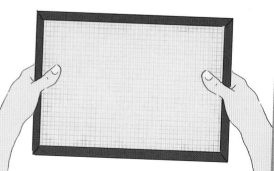

3 Let the water drain out, then carefully place the soggy paper sheet onto a woollen cloth. Put another cloth on top and pile up lots of layers of paper sheets and cloths.

4 Use a heavy pressing machine to squeeze out the water. This squishes the cotton fibres together too.

5 Separate the cloths and take out the sheets of paper to dry in a heated room.

6 You can **buff** the paper with a stone to make it really smooth.

This process took a lot of work and time! That's why paper was a luxury 300 years ago.

MAKING PAPER – IN A FACTORY

Nowadays 400 million tonnes of paper are made every year, and more than a million tonnes are used every day! The only way to make this much paper is in factories. Today we use wood pulp instead of cotton.

A paper-making machine is huge – normally about twice the length of a football pitch! It has seven sections.

1 Headbox: this brings in the porridgy stock made from wood pulp and water. The wood fibres have been smashed up so they will stick together.

2 Wire section: a conveyor belt of mesh up to 35 metres long. The stock is spread over the whole mesh. The water drains off and is sucked away.

3 Press section: huge rollers squeeze the paper to remove more water. Felts (pads similar to blankets) protect the paper.

4 Drier section: 40–70 heated cylinders dry the paper.

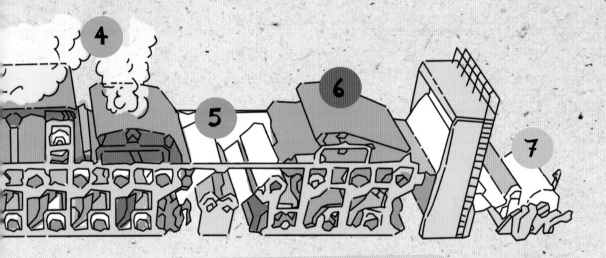

5 Size press: partway through the drying process, a mixture of water and clay or chalk can be added. This makes the surface better for printing on.

6 Calendar: a stack of polished iron rollers smooth the paper's surface, a bit like ironing.

7 Reel: the paper is rolled up at a speed of about 100 kilometres per hour! A reel can hold around 30 tonnes of paper.

PAPER MONEY

A few paper factories make a very special sort of paper – money! The factories usually belong to the government. China was probably the first country to use paper money, starting about a thousand years ago. Now every country has its own notes.

People work hard to make sure it is very difficult to copy the printing on a banknote. Look at some of the security features on an English note:

raised print that you can feel with your fingers

metallic thread woven through the paper

thick paper which 'feels right'

watermark – hold the note up to the light to see it

hologram – the image changes when you tilt it

NOTES AROUND THE WORLD

Some countries have vertical banknotes. Sri Lankan ones are printed horizontally on one side and vertically on the other.

South Africa's banknotes feature images of local wildlife.

Often banknotes show people, buildings or places that are important to their country's history.

NO MORE PAPER?

Countries are introducing banknotes made of plastic. They will not get torn and will last longer than paper banknotes.

FOLDING PAPER

Anyone can fold a piece of paper, right? So really, anyone should be able to make a whole range of things out of paper. You can make them just by folding – no scissors, no glue.

You could make ...

a crane

a frog

a butterfly

a flower

a boat

... or hundreds of other things.

WHAT'S IN A NAME?

Most people call paper-folding 'origami'. That's a Japanese word. Guess what it means? 'Ori' = fold, 'kami' = paper. Yes!

Sounds cooler in Japanese, though, doesn't it?

People are still designing new ways of folding paper, and new things to make. Here are some brilliant examples of modern origami.

Others use lots of pieces of paper rather than just one.

Some people wet the paper they are folding to change the shapes they can make.

Some people even fold money!

HOW OLD IS ORIGAMI?

People can't quite decide! It may have started in Japan or China. Some people think origami must be as old as paper. But there is no proof. The first piece of writing that mentions paper-folding is less than 400 years old.

13

FOLDING PAPER – MAKE A CRANE

Do you think you could make 1000 of these in a year? According to Japanese tradition, if you do, a wish you make should come true.

1 Start with a square piece of paper. Fold it in half diagonally.

2 Unfold the paper and then fold it diagonally the other way.

3 Unfold it and turn it over.

4 Fold the paper in half to make a rectangle. Unfold it and fold the other way.

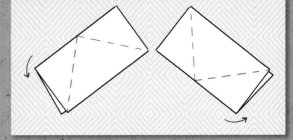

5 Hold the folded paper and bring your fingers and thumbs together to bring the four corners together. Flatten the folded paper so two flaps are pointing each way.

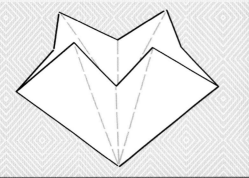

6 Fold the two edges of the top flap into the middle.

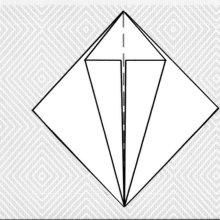

7 Now fold the top corner down and crease it well. Unfold steps 6 and 7.

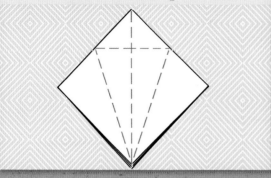

8 Lift the bottom corner of the top layer, so that the sides meet in the centre, and fold down flat.

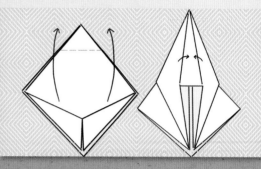

9 Repeat steps 6–8 with the other side, then put the paper with two points towards you.

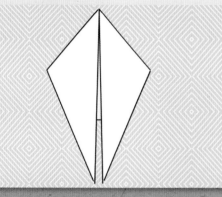

10 Fold in the two outside edges to meet in the middle and repeat this on the other side.

11 Pull the point at one side inside out and fold it like this. Do the same on the other side.

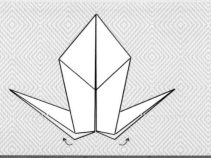

12 Fold the top of one point inside out again, to make the crane's head. Pull the wings out to finish the crane.

Now make another 999! (Or is that wish really so important?)

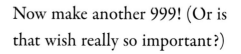

PAPER ENGINEERING

Paper engineering is all about making paper move! No, not by throwing it across a room (we'll come to that later). It's about designing and making moving paper items like models or pop-ups. A paper engineer called 'Bag of Badgers' told me about his job.

Q: What was the first thing you made?

A: It was a pop-up model of a historic windmill.

Q: How long have you been a paper engineer?

A: I first tried it at art school, but I've been working solely as a paper engineer for seven years.

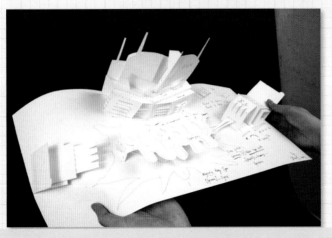

Q: What stages does a project go through, from start to finish?

A: It takes a lot of thinking before I even get started. Then loads of drawings and **dummy models** to make sure things work. Whenever I hit a problem, I have to think up a way around it and make a new dummy. My favourite part is seeing the finished piece.

Q: How long does it take to make a project?

A: It always takes longer than I expect. Sometimes less than a day — or up to two months.

Q: What's the worst thing about being a paper engineer?

A: When things don't work as they should.

Q: And what's the best thing?

A: Making fun things — and that's the whole job!

BE A PAPER ENGINEER!

To make a pop-up card you will need:

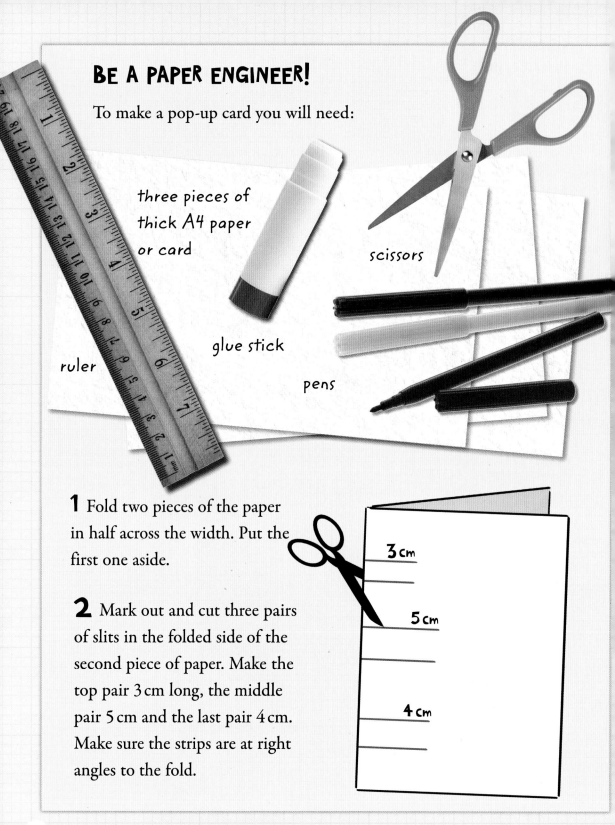

three pieces of thick A4 paper or card

scissors

glue stick

pens

ruler

1 Fold two pieces of the paper in half across the width. Put the first one aside.

2 Mark out and cut three pairs of slits in the folded side of the second piece of paper. Make the top pair 3 cm long, the middle pair 5 cm and the last pair 4 cm. Make sure the strips are at right angles to the fold.

3 cm

5 cm

4 cm

3 Open the card and push the strips inside. Make sure you get the whole length through, and fold the paper down.

Now open the card – the folds should stick out towards you.

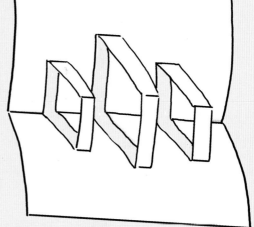

4 Cut three shapes from the third piece of paper. On one, write 'Happy Birthday!' On the second, draw a picture. On the third, write 'From' and your name. Stick them to the folds you have made to pop up.

5 Now draw a design on the outside of the other folded piece of paper.

6 Lastly, put glue on the back of the paper with the pop-ups. Stick it carefully inside the other folded piece of paper to complete your card.

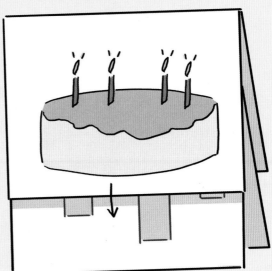

PAPER CUTTING

This art form started in China about 1500 years ago. Like origami, the basic idea is very simple. You cut away all the bits that aren't part of your picture. Hmm, that doesn't sound so easy ...

LADY MARY S. L. BRIDGEMAN.

THE HON. GEORGE T. O. BRIDGEMAN.

In Europe in the 1800s, people cut paper portraits called silhouettes out of black card.

Today, there are paper-cutting artists all over the world.

The British artist, Rob Ryan, is possibly the most famous paper cutter. His works include words as well as images.

The Danish artist, Peter Callesen, often uses a single sheet of white paper and models the paper he cuts away to create a sculpture.

HOW IT'S DONE

First the artist draws their design really carefully on a piece of paper. So that no pencil marks will show, they draw on the back. This means they need to draw a mirror image of what they want, which can be tricky if the picture includes words!

Then they use a sharp craft knife to cut away the parts they don't want.

They work on a special cutting mat so they don't damage the table or blunt the craft knife too quickly. They are also very careful when using the sharp knife!

PAPER IN CELEBRATIONS

Paper is used in celebrations all over the world.

In the United States of America (USA), there are sometimes 'ticker-tape parades'. People throw paper from the windows of tall buildings onto a procession in the streets. They used to throw long strings of paper called 'ticker tape', which was used in office machines before computers were invented.

You can see the long strings of tape in this parade.

The very first ticker-tape parade was held in New York in October 1886, to celebrate the Statue of Liberty being completed. In 1969, the Apollo astronauts who landed on the Moon were given a ticker-tape parade. You can see the paper is different – just shredded paper and confetti – because ticker tape had nearly gone out of use by then.

In Mexico's Day of the Dead celebrations, people make **shrines** to their dead relatives.

They decorate them with gifts of flowers and food – sugar skulls are very popular. They also use tissue paper decorations.

This decorative tissue paper is called *papel picado* in Spanish, meaning **perforated** paper.

About 50 sheets of tissue paper are cut at once, using a very sharp chisel to cut out the design.

Papel picado is very fragile, but this does not matter. Like the flowers and the food on the shrines, it is not meant to last forever, to reflect the life of a person.

LANTERNS

I think these lanterns are some of the most beautiful paper crafts used in celebrations. They glow like little spaceships in the dark! They seem to have been invented in the Far East, but these days people enjoy them all over the world.

!

Some countries have banned sky lanterns because they can cause fires where they land.

HOW SKY LANTERNS WORK

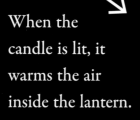

Sky lanterns are made of thin paper stretched over a narrow frame. There's a small candle inside.

Because the paper lantern is so light, this warm, rising air makes it float off the ground.

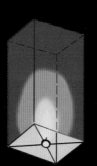

When the candle is lit, it warms the air inside the lantern.

It only comes down when the flame goes out or the whole thing burns away.

FLOATING WATER LANTERNS

These lanterns are Japanese. They look quite like sky lanterns, but they are designed to float on water instead of rising into the air.

Every July or August, during the Obon festival, Japanese people remember those who have died. They believe the spirits of the dead come back to visit them during the festival. On the last day of the festival, people light lanterns and float them on a river. The floating lanterns guide the spirits back to the other world.

RUAS FLORIDAS

This paper-based festival takes place every two years in the small Portuguese town of Redondo. It first happened in 1838. *Ruas floridas* (*say* roo-ahs flo-ree-dahs) means 'flowered streets' but there is so much more than paper flowers to this celebration. Just look at these decorations!

Some streets have ceilings put up, like the one over this windmill.

This street is full of sweet treats.

This whole street was taken over by Alice in Wonderland characters in 2013.

The decorations are taken down after a week, and then the streets have to wait another two years for their next transformation.

RUAS FLORIDAS: HOW DOES IT ALL HAPPEN?

The people who live or work in a particular street start meeting in November or December. They decide on the theme for their street and start secretly working on the plans and making the decorations. Next August, they decorate their street. It's only then that everyone gets to see what's happening in the other streets.

How many streets are decorated?

Between 30 and 40.

RECYCLING PAPER

I love recycling, and guess what – paper is one of the world's most recycled products!

WHY RECYCLE PAPER?

- It saves wood and water.

- Making new paper from old paper takes about half the energy of starting with fresh wood pulp.

- It reduces **pollution**.

- If paper isn't recycled, it gets burnt or buried in landfill sites. Both create more **greenhouse gases** than recycling.

- Around 70% of the **raw material** used in papermaking in the UK is recycled paper.

Recycling one tonne of paper saves roughly 17 trees. The exact amount depends on the type of paper.

WHICH PAPER CAN'T BE RECYCLED?

Paper cannot be recycled endlessly – the fibres get weaker and shorter each time, so it needs to be mixed with new fibre to make good paper. It can actually be recycled up to six times.

Paper that is mixed with food waste or broken glass can't be recycled.

We want to keep some paper for a long time – as books, for example, or on walls as wallpaper.

TRADING PAPER

Paper is made almost everywhere. But Europe and North America between them use about a third of the world's paper, so other countries buy some of their waste paper to recycle. The USA sells nearly half of the paper that they gather for recycling.

RECYCLING PAPER INTO NEW THINGS

Making new paper isn't the only way to recycle paper. Clever people all over the world use waste paper to make new things. Some women in Uganda, Africa, make waste paper into beads. This is how they do it.

There are weekly markets for waste paper. This includes paper where the printing has gone wrong and unsold magazines. Bead-makers mostly buy posters. They look out for the colours they know will make popular beads. They **haggle** with the stallholders to get a good price.

They sort the paper by colour and cut it into strips of different widths. Some are almost the same width all the way along and others are much wider at one end than the other. The women roll the strips of paper, then glue them to create beads. The different widths mean the shapes are varied, making some beads that are wider or chunkier than others. Then the women **varnish** the beads and hang them up to dry.

The women pack up the beads by colour, size and style. They sell them to people who make jewellery in Europe and North America. It's a fairtrade business – the bead-makers are properly paid for their time and effort.

FLYING PAPER

Paper can fly – you can use it to make paper planes! This is my usual style. My big brother taught it to me.

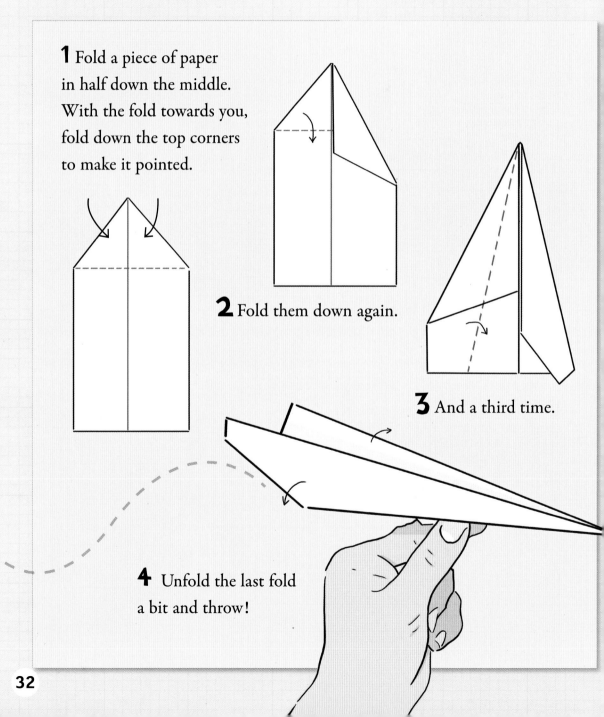

1 Fold a piece of paper in half down the middle. With the fold towards you, fold down the top corners to make it pointed.

2 Fold them down again.

3 And a third time.

4 Unfold the last fold a bit and throw!

This paper plane is completely different. It's a cylinder and doesn't look like a plane at all.

1 Fold over 1 cm on the long end of a piece of paper.

2 Fold it over again and again, until there is about 7 cm left.

3 Carefully roll the paper into a tube with the folded part on the outside. Tape it down the join without squashing it.

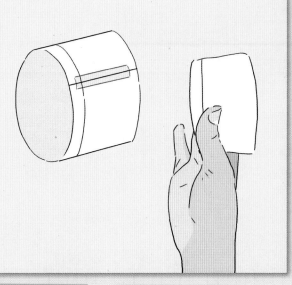

4 Now hold it with the thick end away from you and throw it directly forwards. (If your hands are quite small, start with your fingers inside.)

RECORD-BREAKING PLANE

Record set: Biggest paper aircraft
Time and place: September 2013, in Germany
Wingspan: 18.2 metres
Amount of paper: 70 square metres
Length of flight: 18 metres

BUILDING WITH PAPER

Have you ever made a model building out of paper? This tiny cathedral is made of card and it's over 150 years old.

A model-maker called William Gorringe made this and 27 other cathedrals in the mid-1800s. Some of the pieces of card are so tiny it is hard to believe they were cut by hand.

Small models of buildings are amazing, but did you know that paper products are used as building materials in full-size structures?

CANTERBURY CATHEDRAL

Actual height: 76 m   Model height: 10.5 cm

Actual length: 157 m   Model length: 21.8 cm

LIFE-SIZE STRUCTURES

Paper is often used in building: recycled paper can be used for insulation, and paper screens that divide rooms are traditionally used in Japanese houses. But could someone make a whole structure out of paper?

Yes – by using cardboard tubes. They are surprisingly strong! They can even be made waterproof and fireproof.

The Japanese architect, Shigeru Ban, is famous for creating structures using cardboard tubes.

I love this bridge which he built over the Gardon river in France. It was only designed to last for one summer – but 20 people could stand on it at a time! That's how strong cardboard tubes can be.

But could a whole building be made of cardboard?

BUILDINGS FOR DISASTER AREAS

Shigeru Ban is also famous for creating buildings for people who lose their homes (refugees) in a **crisis**. His emergency structures are fast and cheap to build, practical and often beautiful too.

Ban's early refugee shelters in Rwanda, Africa, used paper tubes instead of tree trunks or **aluminium** poles. This saved trees and money.

Chengdu, in China, was hit by an earthquake in 2008. Ban designed a new school for the children there. His team of students was able to build nine classrooms in a single month! Despite another earthquake, the school is still standing and being used.

In 2011, Canterbury in New Zealand suffered a huge earthquake. Shigeru Ban designed this new cathedral. You can see the cardboard tubes in the walls and roof structure.

WHY USE CARDBOARD IN A CRISIS?

Cardboard is made all over the world, so it can always be found locally. In a crisis, lots of things have to be brought in: people to help, medicines, food, so it's good to be able to use materials that are already made in the area.

And when they're no longer needed, the buildings can be taken apart and recycled!

From decorations to money to buildings, there's not much you can't make with paper. And then you can recycle it and start again. Pretty good stuff, isn't it?

GLOSSARY

aluminium: a strong, light metal

buff: to polish or shine

crisis: a bad situation

dummy models: rough versions of a model, made to test whether it works properly

greenhouse gases: gases like carbon dioxide, which contribute to climate change

haggle: try to lower the price

mesh: material that is made like a net, with holes between the threads

perforated: with lots of holes in it

pollution: bringing harmful substances into nature

pulp: soft, wet substance

raw material: the most basic form that something is made out of

shrine: a collection of objects to help remember someone

starch: special product that makes materials stiffer

stuff: a mixture of cotton fibres, water and starch that was used to make paper by hand

varnish: to coat with something that dries as a hard, shiny surface

INDEX

ABOUT THE AUTHOR

I am a writer and editor. I've written about 20 books and edited more than I can remember. Mostly I write about history, nature and science. Probably the best thing about writing books is learning new things – I get really excited when I find out something zingy. Then I go around telling all my friends, which is probably one reason why they think I'm weird.

I found out so much about paper that we had to make this book longer to fit it all in! There is so much here that excites me, from paper beads to the cardboard bridge. Maybe if I make 1000 origami cranes, I'll get to visit Redondo's flowered streets one day ...

Greg Foot, Series Editor

I've loved science ever since the day I took my papier mâché volcano into school. I filled it with far too much baking powder, vinegar and red food colouring, and WHOOSH! I covered the classroom ceiling in red goo. Now I've got the best job in the world: I present TV shows for the BBC, answer kids' science questions on YouTube, and make huge explosions on stage at festivals!

Working on TreeTops inFact has been great fun. There are so many brilliant books, and guess what ... they're all packed full of awesome facts! What's your favourite?